A Variety Sermon Series

Sermon Outlines For Easy Preaching

Dr. Joseph R. Rogers, Sr.

Introduction

The Preaching of the gospel is a great opportunity to share with the people of God some wonderful and enriching insights that shed a tremendous light unveiling the truths of God.

The word **'PREACH'** means to lecture, to sermonize, to speak or to deliver the message of the Lord Jesus Christ.

The bible speaks loud, clear and with authority as it relates **who must preach** and the **reason for preaching (teaching).**

The Apostle Paul writes to the Romans in chapter ten and said, ***"[15] And how shall they preach, except they be sent? as it is written, How beautiful are the feet of them that preach the gospel of peace, and bring glad tidings of good things"***!

Why must the gospel be preached? The Apostle Paul writes again to the church a **Corinth** and said, ***"But if our gospel be hid, it is hid to them that are lost."*** **(2 Corinthians 4:3)**

So, the Lord Jesus Christ need lips of clay to deliver His message to the lost, as well as to the believer for growth, strength and development.

It is my pray that you will find these short outlines helpful as you go into your **secret closet** (prayer and study time) and **seek** the Lord's guidance as you prepare for those whom He has commissioned you to share this wonderful, timely and relevant message with.

Whatever you do take preaching seriously, in doing so, the Lord will richly bless your efforts as you yield your members to the Holy Ghost.

Be Blessed And Preach The Gospel
Joseph R. Rogers, Sr., D. Min.
Pastor/Teacher

Table Of Contents

Page No.

"The Christian's 'Hymnal'"

A Sermon By Dr. Joseph R. Rogers, Sr.
For The Mount Zion First Baptist Church
Rocky, North Carolina 27804
Theme: The Christian Walk
November 21 2017

Scripture: "**Bless** the Lord, O my soul: and '**all**' that is within me, **Bless** His holy name. **Bless** the Lord, O my soul; and '**forget**' not all **His Benefits**". **(Psalm 103:1,2)**

Introduction

My brothers and my sisters if there are ever to be a happy and joyous people in the world it should be the People of God. You may say, **"why" Brother Pastor?** Well, it is because we are King kids, of great royalty, and we have eternal life as our destiny.

Who is it that would not be happy knowing that whatever 'situation' you get into the Lord will come to your rescue, knowing that whatever 'sickness' comes, the Lord will right there to heal you; just knowing that The Lord is Good All The Time!!

Well, there are some 'songs' in the scriptures that each of us can go to a sing every time we face difficult times—The Psalms!! The Psalms are of different styles depending up the situation the Psalmist found themselves—joy, wanting to be delivered, spiritual guidance, or victory over the adversary.

In other words, some of the Psalms were written for 'praise' and 'devotion', while others for 'prayer' and 'petition', and so on. In this message, we shall pay special attention to those psalms that lend themselves as 'songs of praise'.

Our purpose will be to illustrate how the Book of Psalms can be used by the Christian as a tool **(or "hymnal")** to offer **'joyful praise'** and **'devotion'** to a wonderful and loving God. Let's begin by noticing that there are several "Classes of Psalms" which are geared toward singing Praises to God.

Exposition I

I. PSALMS DESIGNED FOR USE IN 'SINGING PRAISES':

THE MOST OBVIOUS ARE THE "HALLELUJAH" PSALMS. These are psalms beginning and/or ending with "praise" the Lord or "hallelujah". Psalm 148 is an example of this type of psalm. It is often called "The Joy-Song Of Creation" and it has inspired several of our modern songwriters.

For example, the song "Hallelujah, Praise Jehovah". Notice Psalms 146-150 they all begins and ends with **<u>"hallelujah"</u>** or **<u>"praise the Lord"</u>** depending upon your translation.

A SIMILAR GROUP OF PSALMS ARE THOSE CLASSIFIED AS ‘PSALMS OF "PRAISE"’. These psalms of praise are more general in nature and an example would be Psalm 100- “Make a joyful noise unto the Lord, all ye land” (v.1)

This Psalm is described by some as "A Song Of Praise For The Lord's Faithfulness To His People". It is Compare it to the modern song entitled "All People That On Earth Do Dwell".

Another example of a Psalm of Praise is Psalm 8 which says, “O Lord our Lord, how ‘excellent’ is thy name in all the earth! Who has set thy ‘glory’ above the heavens” (v.1).

<u>Exposition II</u>

II. ANOTHER GROUPING ARE THE PSALMS OF "THANKSGIVING":

These psalms are expressions of **‘grateful praise’** to Jehovah and ‘thanksgiving’ to Him for deliverance, greatness, etc."

Some examples are Psalms 100:4,5-“Enter into His ‘gates’ with ‘thanks-giving’ and into His ‘courts’ with ‘praise’: be THANKFUL unto Him, and BLESS His name. For the Lord is good; His mercy is everlasting; and His truth endureth to all generations”.

Another is Psalm 118 in which thanksgiving is offered for the Lord's saving goodness. It let us know that it is better to trust in the Lord than in man. Psalm 118:29-“O give THANKS unto the Lord; for He is good: for His mercy endureth forever”.

Many of the Psalms fall into one of these categories. As such, they lend themselves to singing praises to God. Well, since Christians are commanded to sing Psalms according to Ephesians 5:19; Colossian 3:16; James 5:13, let's consider ways that we can make use of these psalms.

Exposition III

Well, we can use these songs in our worship as well as our devotional services. If they are sung with ‘sincerity’ and ‘truthfulness’ they will bless our souls as well as those who hear them. We can use these by..

1. BY MAKING USE OF THOSE PSALMS ALREADY ARRANGED FOR OUR SINGING: Like those often found in modern songbooks. There are even special hymnals [psalms arranged to fit] the way we sing today (e.g., "Selected Psalms For Church Singing", by C.E.I. Publishing Co.)

2. WE CAN ALSO LEARN TO READ THE PSALMS OF PRAISE AND THANKSGIVING WITH AN "ATTITUDE OF JOYFUL PRAISE". If we have our Bibles, we can still offer up ‘praises’ to God by using the ‘Book of Psalms’ as a "hymnal"! Some examples are:

Psalm 9:1-“I will praise thee, O Lord with my whole heart: I will shew forth all thy marvelous works”.

Psalm 15:1-“Lord who shall abide in thy tabernacle? Who shall dwell in thy holy hill?”

Psalm 18:1,2a-“I will love thee, O Lord, My strength. The Lord is my rock, and my fortress; my God, my strength...etc.”.

Psalm 24:1-“The earth is the Lord’s, and the fulnes thereof; the world, and they that dwell therein”.

Psalms 27:1-“The Lord is my light and my salvation; who shall I fear. The Lord is the strength of my life; of who shall I be afraid”.

Psalm 34:1-“I will bless the Lord at all times: His praise shall continually be in my mouth”.

Psalm 46:1-“God is our refuge and strength, a very present help in trouble”.

Psalm 66:1,2-“Make a joyful noise unto the Lord all ye land; sing forth the honor of his name; make his praise glorious.

Psalm 90:1-“Lord, thou hast been our dwelling place in all generations”.

Psalm 92:1-“It is a good thing to give thanks unto the Lord, and to sing praises unto thy name, O Most High”.

Psalm 95:1-“O Come, let us sing unto the Lord: let us make a joyful noise to the rock of our salvation”.

<u>Psalm 96:1</u>-"O Sing unto the Lord a new song: sing unto the Lord, all ye earth".

<u>Psalm 146:1,2</u>-"Praise ye the Lord. Praise ye the Lord, O my soul. While I live will I praise the Lord: I will sing praise unto my God while I have any being".

<u>Psalm 149:1</u>-"Praise ye the Lord. Sing unto the Lord a new song, and His praise in the congregation of saints".

<u>Psalms 150:1</u>-"Praise ye the Lord. Praise God in his sanctuary; praise him in the firmament of his power".

Conclusion

So, as I close this message brothers and sisters I am so glad that I am able to sing unto the Lord with 'praise' and **'gladness'** making melody with my heart unto Him.

So, it is my hope that we come to **'appreciate'** the Book of Psalms as they were originally intended, that is, to be a collection of songs, specifically designed to be offered in 'praise' and 'worship' to the Lord.

Once we learn this, we will then be able to do what Hymn Number 150:2-6 stanzas which says, Praise Him…"**For His mighty acts**", "**According to his excellent greatness**",

"**With the sound of the trumpet**",

"**With the psaltery and harp**",

"**With the timbrel and dance**",

"**With the stringed instruments and dance**",

"**Upon the loud cymbals**",

"**Upon the High Sounding cymbals**",

Let **'EVERYTHING' (that includes you and me)** that 'hath' **breath (life) 'PRAISE'** YE THE LORD. **PRAISE YE THE LORD.**

"**The Christian's 'Hymnal'**"
Dr. Joseph R. Rogers, Sr.
Mount Zion First Baptist Church
Rocky Mount, NC 27904

"The Lord Is My Shepherd-#1"

A Sermon By Dr. Joseph R. Rogers, Sr
For The Mount Zion First Baptist Church
Rocky Mount, North Carolina 27804
Theme: The Lord Is My Shepherd
November 5, 2017

Scripture: "[1] The Lord [is] my shepherd (protector); [I] [shall] not want (be in need)". (Psalm 23:1)

Is = a verb that suggest that a person, place of things remains, stands, stays!
Shall = going to, abut to, intend to

Introduction

My brothers and sisters as we come to "unfold" and "unveil" this magnificent and wonderful song of David, it is wonderful know that it is most though of during times of death and bereavement; yet this is a very "personal" (I, my me & mine) and "intimate" (The Lord Is, right now and will there forever be) writing of 'comfort' and 'encouragement'.

I love (Psalm 1)- "Blessed is the man that walketh not in the counsel of the ungodly nor standeth in way of sinners."

I love (Psalm 27)- "The Lord is my light and my salvation; whom shall I fear? the Lord is the strength of my life; of whom shall I be afraid."

I Love (Psalm 34)- "I will bless the Lord at all times: his praise shall continually be in my mouth".

I love (Psalm 37)- "Fret not thyself because of evildoers, neither be thou envious against the workers of iniquity".

I love (Psalm 100)- "Make a joyful noise unto the Lord, all ye lands."

I love (Psalm 103)- "Bless the Lord, O my soul: and all that is within me, bless his holy name".

I love (Psalms 150)- "Praise ye the Lord. Praise God in his sanctuary: praise him in the firmament of his power".

Of the seven (7) songs that I have mentioned Psalm 23 is the most quoted of them all (150). It is Psalm 23 is 'Personal' and has been quoted during very challenging times in our lives…

- It has been and is recited by the -bedside- of loved ones as they enter their final days or hours on earth.

- It has been and is recited when people find themselves in -need of blessings- for the Lord.

- It has been and is recited when people find themselves in a -spiritual battle- with the Devil

This Psalm has been ascribed as the penmanship of King David because of his relationship with the Lord and in his quest to do the Master's will.

In his early life, God anointed David to be King of Israel, after King Saul disobeyed Him in not destroying all of Amalekites.

"[3] *Now go and smite Amalek, and utterly destroy all that they have, and spare them not; but slay both man and woman, infant and suckling, ox and sheep, camel and ass"*. (1 Samuel 15:3)

Later, King David was not allowed to build the "Temple" because of his sin with Bathsheba and killing her husband (Uriah). His son Solomon was granted that privileges, therewith naming it, “The Temple of Solomon”

It has been suggested David wrote this song during the high of his military career as a mighty man of valor.

In that, when Saul’s Army was gripped with fear in the Valley of Elah. There David a lad, just from watching over the flock of his father, Jesse, accepted the challenge of the Giant Goliath.

As the army of Saul postured themselves in ‘fear’, already had on his resume’, The slewing of Lion and killing the Bear, said who is this uncircumcised Philistine, that defy The Lord God!

Well, the story ends with The Lad David, killing Goliath with a sling and a smooth stone. In this same vein, David pens a powerful writing to encourage you and I in our struggles in life.

Psalms 23 is a song of faith, trust, assurance and confidence. It expresses assured confidence in God's power, blessings and goodness not only in the life to come, but also NOW!

Psalms 23 offers some wholesome spiritual insights that are so uplifting that one can feel nothing be encouragement in whatever situation they might find themselves.

This Psalm speaks in a personal way about how wonderful the shepherd cares for the sheep. This Psalm adds a brilliant imagery of God's soothing guidance and the ensuing confidence as one is going through battles. Why is the 'flavor' of this song so personal? Well, it speaks in a personal posture…

- ✓ My, "The Lord is [my] shepherd…"
- ✓ I, "[I] shall not want…"
- ✓ Me, "He maketh [me] to lie down in green pastures…"
- ✓ Mine, "Thou preparest a table before [me] in the presence of [mine] Enemies…"

The Psalmist identified himself as **'sheep'** and God as his **<u>'shepherd'</u>**. God is Shepherd because He is the only True guider, supplier and source to/in which the sheep can look to and depend upon.

Today, we are 'sheep', and must understand and accept the fact that without Him (Shepherd) we are doomed for failure, defeat and demise. But, if we rest in the Shepherd's hand; the sheep we are care for, comforted, guarded, protected and blessed.

In the words of this text the sheep are taught to express their satisfaction in the Great Mighty Pastor of the universe; this Redeemer and this Preserver of all men.

And with **'joy'** today we as David should express joy that our Shepherd is powerful, loving and caring. This is why He is described in so many ways! "Jehovah". (Yahweh, Elyon, El)

What does "Jehovah" mean?

Jehovah-Jireh = Lord Provider- Philip 4:19

Jehovah-Nissi = Lord My Banner = I Chronicles 29:11-13

Jehovah-Shalom = Lord My Peace – Isa. 9:6, Rom 8:31-35

Jehovah-Tsidkenu = Lord My Righteousness - I Cor 1:30

Jehovah-Tsori (tory) = Lord My Strength - Psalm 19:14

All of these names only suggest: The Lord is my Shepherd (my comforter, my guide, my supplier and my strength) and I shall not want (be in lack, or be in need, to be in want or have not)

Exposition I

The twenty-third Psalm is the most familiar and best songs of all Scripture in the bible. It has a way of soothing the spirits of one who sees the death angel, telling them and their loved ones that physical death is not final, it is but a transition from…

- **“mortal” to “immortality”,**
- **“labor” to “reward”,**
- **“sadness” to “joy”**
- **“tears” to “jubilation”**

Knowing that ‘physical death’ no longer has victory. Because of the shedding of the blood of Jesus, ‘death’ has no more sting and the ‘grave’ has no more “victory”.

The main theme of the foundation of our focus today, illustrates one of the names aforementioned, for God. "Jehovah-Rohi" = The Lord is my shepherd!

There is no greater relationship in the bible than that of the Shepherd and Sheep. It shows that even though one can be facing the final common denominator of life, "death"; yet there is still 'HOPE' in Jesus Christ! Saints who die in the Lord can say with enthusiasm, "The Lord Is My Shepherd".

I. "The Lord Is My Shepherd…etc.": (Guide; Overseer; Protector)

In the Old Testament, Sheep died for the Shepherd. In the New Testament, Shepherd dies for the Sheep. The Lord Jesus Christ is our Three-Fold Shepherd.

a. The **"good"** shepherd. (John 10:11)
b. The "great" shepherd. (Hebrews 13:20)
c. The **"chief"** shepherd. (1 Peter 5:4)

- a. He died to **"save"** the sheep, that's -Salvation-.

- b. He lives to **"keep"** the sheep, that's -Security-.

c. He is coming to **<u>“reward”</u>** the sheep that’s -<u>Service-.</u>

As Sheep, we are His Prize. The **“nature” and “habits”** of sheep make them different from most other animals. They are prone to wander off. They cannot protect themselves. Sheep need ‘guides’ and ‘protectors’.

As Sheep, we are:
a. The Property of God.
b. Purchased by His sacrifice and blood.
c. Priceless (more valuable than silver or gold).

Psalm 100:3-"KNOW YE THAT THE LORD HE IS GOD: IT IS HE THAT HATH MADE US, AND NOT WE OURSELVES; WE ARE HIS PEOPLE, AND THE SHEEP OF HIS PASTURE."

My brothers and sisters, we are His...We Identified with him. There are **no "if's", "but's", or "I hope so's".**

Psalm 18:2-"THE LORD IS MY ROCK, AND MY FORTRESS, AND MY DELIVERER; MY GOD, MY STRENGTH, IN WHOM I WILL TRUST; MY BUCKLER, AND THE HORN OF MY SALVATION, AND MY HIGH TOWER."

King David remined us that, "The Lord Is My Shepherd". Now, the second half of this sentences assures us that, in being our Shepherd, there are some fringed benefits: "I Shall Not Want".

Exposition II

II. I Shall Not Want:
(Be In Need Of Anything)

A. I shall not want for what? Our Shepherd's…

1. 'Riches' are unsearchable.
2. 'Joys' is unspeakable.
3. 'Powers' is unlimited.
4. 'Faithfulness' is unfailing.
5. 'Words' is unshakable.
6. 'Loves' is unchanging.

Yes, my brothers and sisters,

- When the toils of challenges come,
- When things are lacking or empty and…
- When wolves of life come…we can say the second part of our

text for today, **"I SHALL NOT WANT.**

Why? Because the ‘True Shepherd’, The Lord Jesus Christ is forever our ‘guide’ and ‘comforter’.

I shall not…

1. For **“health”,** because, "With His stripes we are healed." (Isaiah 53:3), and Jesus "Himself took our infirmities, and bare our sickness." **(St. Matthew 8:17).**

2. For **“prosperity”,** because "My God shall supply all your need according to His riches in glory by Christ Jesus." **(Philippians 4:19).**

3. For **“security”**, because, "God has not given us the spirit of fear; but of power, and of love, and of a sound mind." **(II Timothy 1:7).**

4. For **“faith”**, because, "God hath dealt to every man the measure of faith." **(Romans 12:3).**

5. For **“peace”,** for "Thou wilt keep him in perfect peace, whose mind is stayed on Thee: because he trusteth in Thee." **(Isaiah 26:3).**

6. For **“victory”**, because, "Nay, in all these things we are more than conquerors through Him that loved us." **(Romans 8:37).**

8. For **“victory over confusion”** because, "God is not the author of confusion, but of peace." **(1 Corinthians 14:33).**

9. For **“companionship”** because, Jesus said, "Lo, I am with you always, even unto the end of the world." **(Matthew 28:20).**

10. For **‘contentment’**, because, "For I have learned in whatsoever state (or circumstance) I am therewith to be content." **(Philippians 4:11).**

11. For **“victory over the cares of this life’**, because, I am casting all my care upon Him who cares for me. **(I Peter 5:7).**

12. For **“victory in prayer”**, because, for if we ask anything in Jesus' name we shall have it. **(John 14:14).**

13. For “strength”, because, "The Lord is the strength of my life of whom shall I be afraid" (Psalms 27:1).

14. For **“power”**, because "Ye shall receive power, after that the Holy Ghost is come upon you." **(Acts 1:8)**

15. To be an **“over-comer”**, because, Jesus said, "In the world ye shall have tribulation: but be of good cheer, I have overcome the world." **(John 16:33).**

16. For “victory over persecution”, because, "If God be for us, who can be against us?" **(Romans 8:31).**

17. For **“liberty”,** because, "Where the spirit of the Lord is, there is liberty." **(II Corinthians 3:17).**

18. For **“wisdom”,** because, Christ Jesus is made unto me wisdom from God. **(1 Corinthians 1:30).**

19. For “ability”, because, "I can do all things through Christ which strengtheneth me." **(Philippians 4:13).**

20. For “joy”, because, the joy of the Lord is my strength. (Nehemiah 8:10), and with joy shall I draw water out of the wells of salvation. **(Isaiah 12:3).**

21. For “blessings” because, we are blessed "With all spiritual blessings in

heavenly places in Christ." **(Ephesians 1:3).**

22. For **"redemption"** because, I have been redeemed through his blood. **(Ephesians 1:7).**

23. For an "inheritance" because, through him we obtained an inheritance. **(Ephesians 1:11).**

24. For **"position"** because, He (Jesus) has "Made us to sit together in heavenly places in Christ Jesus." **(Ephesians 2:6).**

"The Lord Is My Shepherd""

Dr. Joseph R. Rogers, Sr., Servant Leader
Mont Zion Frist Baptist Church
Rocky Mount, North Carolina 27804

<u>"Weapons Of Mass Destruction"</u>

A Sermon By Joseph R. Rogers, Sr.
For The Mount Zion First Baptist Church
Rocky Mount, North Carolina 27804
Theme: Spiritual Weapons
November 12, 2017

<u>Scripture</u>: "3 For though we **walk -in- the**
flesh, (human nature) we do not **war -**
after- the flesh (engage in battle) 4 (for
the **weapons of our warfare are not**
carnal, but mighty through God to the
pulling down of strongholds (grips of
evil) 5 Casting down **imaginations, (minds,**
thoughts) and **every high thing** that
exalteth itself against the **knowledge of**
God, and bringing into **captivity every**
thought to the **obedience of Christ." (2**
Corinthians 10: 3-5)

"For we **wrestle (engage in battle) not against** flesh and blood, **(humanity)** [but] **against principalities, against powers, against rulers of the darkness of this world, against spiritual wickedness in high places" (Ephesians 6:12)**

<u>Introduction</u>

It is without question that you and I are **indirect victims** of circumstances when it comes to The **'Uprising'** that caused **The Angel Lucifer** and his band of Angels to rebel in Heaven against the Creator, **The God of Abraham, Isaac and Jacob.**

Lucifer was the **Chief Angelic Worship Leader**, therewith, leading that Great Angelic Choir that gave **praise, glory and honor** unto The Lord Our God.

But, because of his **'pride'** and **'quest'** for power and position' he thought He should be equal or had more powerful than **"The Almighty God"**. I was **spiritual suicide** for Him to think He had the power greater than the One who created him. Only God is **all powerful, all knowing** and **everywhere at all times**.

Well, God responded by **casting Satan** and a third of the angelic host that followed Him from Heaven and they have been assigned their eternal punishment, which will commence after that great

Battle of Armageddon which was consummate the worlds as we know it today.

Jude 1:6-"[6] And the **angels** which kept not their first estate, but **left their own habitation**, he hath -**reserved**- in everlasting chains under darkness unto the judgment of the great day".

After Lucifer and these angles were kicked out of Heaven and they **landed on Earth**, and now they go about **deceiving** humanity as they did Adam and Eve in the Garden. This act bought and caused **[SIN]** to reign among the ranks of humanity.

[SIN] is **powerful** and **devastating**; and human intellect is **unable to conquer over IT**. It is only through Jesus Christ that humanity can be 'saved or delivered'.

In order to do **battle with Satan** we must **equip ourselves** with **SPIRITUAL WEAPONS–The Word, The Spirit, Faith And Hope!** Even though Satan has power, yet his activities are still subject to the POWER OF GOD.

The battle that we are engaged is **spiritual not carnal**. The second reference text says, **Ephesian 6:12**-"[12] For we wrestle (engage) not against flesh and blood, but against principalities, against powers, against rulers of the darkness of this world, against spiritual wickedness in high places".

It is **'Satan'** desire to **'interrupt'** and **'destroy'** the lives of humanity that has hope in God. Thanks, be unto the Lord, who has designed and equipped all the believers with, **"Weapons of Mass Destruction".**

A **weapon of mass destruction** (WMD or WoMD) is a **nuclear, radiological, chemical, biological weapon** that can kill and bring significant harm to a **large number of humans** or **cause great damage to human-made structures** (e.g. buildings), **natural structures** (e.g. mountains), or the **biosphere (environment, planet, earth, land, sea and atmosphere).**

Beloved, our weapons are not **knives**, **guns**, **intimidation**, **fear** or **aggression**. Our weapons are **spiritual, mighty in God**

through the pulling down of strong holds."

<u>**Exposition I**</u>

The two texts share with us the **"power"** and **"importance"** of possessing this **Spiritual Weaponry.** Throughout history other generations have used different kinds of weapons:

*The **Egyptians** had their wheeled chariot.

*The **Philistines** had their steel blade.

*The **Romans** had their Legions (Army).

*The **American Civil War** had its repeating rifles.

* In **World War II** had its atomic bomb and…

*The **Middle East** had its **Weapons of Mass Destructions.**

Although, the above is powerful, and have there place in history; yet they are not **comparable** to the **'Spiritual weapons of Mass Destruction'** that I am talking about.

Without a doubt the **Christian Church** is engaged in **warfare,** and she has **"Powerful Spiritual Weapons"** that are able to get the job done. In that same vein let me **admonish** all of us seated in the church today!

It is time out for **Church Members, Church Disciples, Christian Believers** to continue to **engage** in **destroying, harming** and **battling against** each other.

We are **brothers and sisters** we are a FAMILY, and we should be doing everything within our God given **powers and abilities** to assist the fellowship, **Mount Zion First Baptist Church** to achieve her God given destiny.

- **This Fellowship is a "city"** that sits on a hill that offers guidance to those who are need of directions.

- **This Fellowship is <u>"salt"</u>** that flavors the attitudes of those who are in need of counsel and encouragement.

- **This Fellowship is a <u>"hospital"</u>** to those who are in need care and moment of recuperation.

What are our weapons? Well the Scriptures plainly describes them in simple form:

****The Word!** (That us Sharper than any double-edged sword

****The Spirit!** (That is More powerful than TNT, nitro, nuclear bomb)

****Faith!** (That Can climb, tunnel through and move rugged mountains)

****Hope!** (That Will crush all manner of doubt and fear)

The Apostle Paul in this writing to the church at Corinth remind them that their **struggles**, **battles** and **wars** were not against each other, but against the **"Devil".**

In verse five he clarifies that the war is **'against'** the **manifestations of evil imaginations, ungodly principalities and satanic activities**. But, in spite of that very fact…

The Lord has the **"perfect plan"** for victory and when we **implement** and **apply** it correctly, **VICTORY IS ASSURED.** In our spiritual battle…

- ✓ The **pastor** is the commanding general!
- ✓ The **deacons** are the Joint Chiefs of staff!
- ✓ The **presidents/chairs** are the company commanders! and
- ✓ The other **disciples** are infantrymen/women!

You see, all of us must make sure that this ship (Mt Zion First Baptist Church) continue to stand **strong**, **relevant** and **generationally apt** to do the Master's Will.

The Apostle Paul emphasized that the Church needs to be aware of the **nature of the warfare**. This war has never and is not now an internal battle putting…

- ✓ **Deacons** against the preacher, or
- ✓ **Choir members** against the director,
- ✓ **Young folks** against old folks,
- ✓ **Educated** against the uneducated,
- ✓ The **Well to do**, against the **Not so well of–No!**

This battle and war is against **sin, hopelessness, despair, poverty, ignorance, discrimination, spiritual and physical lack, oppression, depression, and carnality that is eating at the chore or foundation of who we are and what we are about.**

Every Christian should remember that there is a war going on; and therefore, we must not forget to **renew our commitment** (Revival) and **holdfast to our allegiance** that can be found in the lyrics of the church hymn that I know…
"I'm on the battlefield for my Lord,

(1)

I was alone and idle,
I was a sinner too,
I heard a voice from heaven
Say there is work to do,
I took the Master's hand,
And I joined the Christian band,
I'm on the battlefield for my Lord.

Yes! I'm on the battlefield for my Lord, I promised him that I would serve him till I die, Yes! I'm on the battlefield for my Lord."

Conclusion

So, as I close, what a wonder experience it is to know that even though we're in a **spiritual battle**; we have nothing to **"fear"**.

Because, the **weapons** of our warfare are **“lethal”:** What are they and where are found? The six (6) chapter of The Apostle Paul’s letter to the Ephesian Church: We are to…

***Gird ourselves loins with truth,**

***Put on the breastplate of righteousness,**

***Shod our feet with the preparation of the gospel of peace,**

***Put on the shield of faith before us,**

***Put on the helmet of salvation,**

***Always carrying the Sword of the Spirit (Word)**

Sealing, it all of these with **‘prayer’ and ‘supplication’**.

The most **lethal weapons** that every child of God has in his/her possession is **“faith and hope”!**

Faith that say, “No matter how gloomy the forecast, with God we are more than conquerors.

Faith that says, “No matter how hard challenge, “I can do all things through Christ that strengtheth me.

Faith that says, No matter the height of life’s mountains and valleys, Ain’t no mountain to high and ain’t no valley to low”.

Faith that says, No matter that size or shape of the weapon, “No weapon that forms itself against me shall prosper”.

Not only is there **FAITH**, there is also “**HOPE**”!

Hope is **Expectation, Anticipation, Jubilation and Celebration** that **something good is about to happen**!

That Hope, that prompts us to march on through the wind and the rains of life.

That Hope, that looks beyond the dreary dark clouds of despair and peers through the silver lining of victory.

That Hope, that looks deep into the depths of the midnight sky and declares that, "**Weeping endures for a night, but joy comes in the morning.**"

The record gives us examples of these weapons being used!

- ✓ **Daniel** used them in the lion's den,
- ✓ **Three Hebrew Boys** used them in the fiery furnace,
- ✓ **Prophet Elijah** used them on Mt Carmel with the prophets of Baal,
- ✓ **Queen Esther** used when she went before the king,
- ✓ **Job** used them when he was turned over to the devil,

They all proved that, **"Our God is an awesome God and that He reins in heaven above". Our God is an awesome God**!

I like the way the hymn writer couched it, ***"It is no secret what God can do, what he's done for others, he'll do for you. with arms wide open, he'll pardon you, it is no secret what God can do."***

Gird yourself with Armor of God:

- **The Word, that equips us!**
- **The Spirit, that guides us!**
- **Faith, that encourages us!**
- **Hope,**

With **these weapons** there is no Devil in hell that will ever **'defeat'** or **'overthrow'** us.

Satan and his fallen angels **bow** (submit) to the **wonderful, powerful, matchless, unconquerable, adoring, sweet name of Jesus!**

And, it is through Him, (Jesus) that we have Weapons of Mass Destruction that are able to 'conquer' any Mountain, 'endure' any valley and 'cross' any river.

<u>"Weapons Of Mass Destruction"</u>

Dr. Joseph R. Rogers, Sr., Servant Leader
The Mount Zion First Baptist Church
Rocky Mount, North Carolina 27804

"Under New Management"

A Sermon By Dr. Joseph R. Rogers, Sr.
For The Mount Zion First Baptist Church
Rocky Mount, North Carolina 27804
Theme: **Changing/Makes A Difference**
September 17, 2017

Scripture: "Therefore, if any man **be in Christ**, he is a **new creature: old things** are **passed away**; behold, **all things are become new. (2 Corinthians 5:17)**

Introduction

Have you ever passed by and old business that had been around for years and see a sign that said… **"Under New Management?"** It does not necessarily mean that the **old products** are not sold there, but it's just **new people** (principles) now **operated the business**.

"Under New Management" does means that some things are **altogether different**, nor does it **always mean** that what's **different is guaranteed** will be **better**.

Today there are many persons who are **affiliated** with the local church who **professes Christianity; b**ut under **close scrutiny**, some of them are just sending **‘smoke signal’** and do not have on board a **real relations** nor **real fire. (They have a form of godliness—but no POWER)**!

I am aware of the faith that **SALVATION SHOULD NEVER BE BASED UPON ‘WORKS’**; yet I do believe that **AFTER SALVATION OR AFTER BEING BORN AGAIN**, there should some **activity of WORKS**!

The Apostle James attest to this very fact by saying, **“Just believing is not enough, there must be works to anchor one’s faith or faith without works, being alone, is DEAD”.**

I have learned that to **get THE most** out of the **Christian experience, or to fulfill one’s destiny, we must** allow **God to -manage- our lives**, **to be our pilot**, or **to direct our parade.**

When Jesus Christ is in our lives, our **relationship is powerful.** While we may have the **same old name; yet under new management**, suggest that, **"Old things are passed away, and all things are become new"!**

Exposition I

This text focuses on use to be, **Saul of Tarus—an intellectual Christian hater**, now, **The Apostle Paul**, a gospel preacher, as he explains the **regenerating effects** of being **"in Christ."**

A person who is **"in Christ"** goes beyond a **simply acknowledgement of Christ** from their lip! Jesus Christ is **first and foremost** and in their daily agenda!

- ✓ To be **"in Christ"** goes even further than **simply being associated** with the **visible church. "If any man be in Christ,"** simply means to **"partake of His benefits and His sufferings.**

- ✓ To be **'In Christ',** is not only an **outward profession**, but it is an **inward change**, a **purity of heart**, and **cohabitation of The Holy Ghost.**"

- ✓ To be in **"in Christ"** is to place one entire **life in the hands of God** to: **manage, control, direct** and **order.** In Jesus Christ, we are **"new creature" walking in power and victory**; which suggest that **The Holy Spirit is in control** of ones **thinking and actions.**

- ✓ To be **'in Christ'** does not mean that we will be able to **escape some of the pressures of life.** It **does mean** that we will **survive any attack of Satan** and **rise as VICTORS**!

  - **Ahead and not beneath!**
  - **Blessed and Highly favored and not cursed!**
  - **Victor and never victims!**

<u>**Exposition II**</u>

So, what are some of the **characteristics** of being in Jesus Christ or being regenerated in/by the Spirit of God"?

A. Liability or Asset:
(Negative, Positive)

Today, some people are **spiritually bankrupt**. They have an **open account**, but **their balance is "zero".** They are **weak** because, no time is given to **prayer**, **study** and **meditating** upon the Lord!

They are the **victims of Spiritual mismanagement**. They come to the House of The Lord only to fulfill, some kind of **religious appetite**. They always arrived late and what leave early.

1. Our Liabilities:
(Negatives of Being Under New Management)

They include our **fears, failures, frustrations, downs, dark days, lonesome valleys and setbacks**. Each of us have a **liability column in life**. But, thanks be to God there is an **Assets Column...**

2. Our Assets:
(Positives of Being Under New Management)

A **strong prayer life,**
infilling of the Holy Spirit, Bible reading and **bible study, public worship and praise, faith building,** and **fellowship with other saints.**

It is **well documented** that **Saints** who **pray often, read their bibles** and **regularly participate in public worship and praise God** are **stronger, bolder in the faith** and have **less frustration** in **their daily walk with the Lord.** Beloved, **while we're under "New Management", We Need…**

B. Our Spiritual Manager:
(Father, Son & Holy Ghost)

Just as the **'growth'** and **'prosperity'** of a regular business success is determined by the **quality of its management,** so is the **quality of our spiritual lives** impacted in the same way.

Exposition II

In a business, the **manager – promotes- company growth.** It is done through **aggressive/non-aggressive advertisements.** The **approaches** may **be**

different, but the **goal is the same, increase sales and assets.**

In business, the **manager -insures quality service**. In this process management stands behind its **product workmanship**. He/She **guarantees** that food is **tasty**! Parts are of **high quality**! Customers are **treated right**!

In a similar sense, the **quality of our spiritual management abilities** reflects in **our 'worship' and 'praise' as we give to -service-** to God, **our church family** and **fellow man, those outside of the church walls.**

- If **we sing** in the choir, do we **give our best**?
- If **we preach or teach**, do we take **time to prepare**?
- If **we are deacons & Trustees**, do we humbly **serve the people**?
- If we are **members of the congregation**, do we **impact the spirituality of the fellowship**; being an "**assets**" to **external**

activities, such as **mission, outreach and evangelism.**

My brothers and sisters, those who **Mis-manage** their business are those who allow the **quality of their service to depreciate** and become **content** with simply **doing just enough to get by**! So, what is it that makes for **'good managers'**? In business…glad you asked!!

- **A Good Manager** is able to make **"tough decisions"** that **produce results**.
- **A Good Manager** will not allow the **"expenses"** to continue to **outweigh income**.
- **A Good Manager** take **an inventory** and **realize that something must be done** before it's **too late**.

In business, what are some noticeable liabilities: **lack of production**, **unwillingness to apply the team concept**, or a **negative attitude**.

In our church, we must not allow **dead weigh**; it matter not how popular, to be the **order of the day.** If someone is in a position and not preforming their duties—they need to **be removed**!

You see, whatever is causing the loss, **a good manager** must be willing/able to do what is **necessary to eliminate loss (dead weight).**

All cancerous attitudes and work habits will 'infect' and 'affect' the entirety of the body; running the risk of cause it to malfunction.

A good manager are not afraid to make choices like "Joshua": Joshua 24:15 "...choose you this day whom ye will serve;...but as for me and my house, we will serve the LORD."

A good manager is accountable. That is, **they answer** to their **Superior; they know how to follow!** Good Managers are **accountable** for **their actions and they should be rewarded for their accomplishments.**

Spiritually, as Blood Washed Believers, we have a MANAGER—JESUS CHRIST OUR LORD! We are **accountable to follower Our Manager's guidance in** our **day to day operations. Accountability** without the corresponding **responsibility is dangerous.**

Conclusion

So, in closing, I am glad announce today that I am, **'Under New Management".** When I try **to manage** my life I **always ended** up in a **spiritual deficit, on the edge of a spiritual crises** or even **spiritually bankruptcy**!

But, I must submit to you that when **a corporation realizes** they have a **problem beyond** their ability, they **immediately** start looking for a **New Manager**!

Again, I submit to you that if you're out of the ark of safety in relations to Jesus Christ, there is a **"Resume"** in **your mailbox**!

Again, I submit to you that if you have lost your zeal, joy and commitment to Jesus Christ, there is a **"Resume"** in your mailbox!

It has been sent from heaven and the sender—Jesus Christ, wants to apply to be **your new manager**! Someone in the sanctuary today, is saying, **"Who is this applicant"**? **Glad You Ask! His…**

****His Name: "El-Shaddai, The Almighty God"; "Jehovah-Jireh, Alpha and Omega, "The beginning and then end. "Moses's Rod", "The Rose of Sharon", "Ezekiel's Wheel In A Wheel", Ester's Courage, Solomon's Wisdom, Jerimiah's Bomb, David's Sling Shot, "Abraham's Sacrifice",**

****<u>His Address</u>**: He live **everywhere**, the -earth- is **his footstool** and the -heavens- are **surround His shoulders**.

- If you take the **wings of the morning** and **fly in the sky or move to the bottomless deep, He is there**!

- If you **ascend into heaven** or even **make your bed in hell, He is there!**

His Phone No: Simply dial area **code 111-PRAY. One** for the father! **One** for the Son! **One** for the Holy Ghost. **"Jesus is on the mainline, tell him what you want and his line is never busy!"**

His Prior Employment:

- **He created the universe!**
- **He put the galaxies in sky!**
- **He formed man from the dust of the earth!**
- **He hollowed out the valleys and**
- **He bulged out the mountains!**
- **He sends the rain and sunshine!**

His Character **References:

- **1 John 4:16**-"He is love.",
- **1 John 1:5**-""He is light; in him there is no darkness",
- **St. John 14:6**-"He is the way the truth and the life".

- **St. John 8:32**-“He us the truth that shall make you free!
- **Philippians 4:19**_”He will shall supply all your need!”
- **Jeremiah 8:22**-"He is our balm in Gilead?
- **Exodus 17:6**-“He is our water from a rock”.

His Availability:

He is willing to **step in your life** and **put things back together again**. He will -**build- your assets**, -**cut down- your liabilities** and bring you into **spiritual balance**, giving you -**abundantly life-** beyond measure!

His Salary Requirement:

You don’t have to **worry about what He service charges are.**

- His check was ‘**drawn**’ from the -**bank- of heaven**,
- His check was ‘**written**’ **at Calvary**, and
- His check was ‘**signed**’ **with the -hand- of Jesus!**

No wonder the songwriter declared, **"Jesus paid it all. All to him I owe. Sin had left his crimson stain but he washed it white as snow!"**

When God saves, my brothers and sisters ... He **justifies, sanctifies** and **glorifies…**

And, there is therefore, NO CONDEMNATION to those who are in Christ Jesus...**we are washed by His precious and powerful blood! "**

And, there is therefore, there is NO SEPARATION from His presence…we are signed, sealed and delivered!

The Apostle Paul couches is like this…"For I am therefore persuaded that neither death nor life, nor angels nor principalities nor powers, nor things present nor things to come, nor height nor depth, nor any other created thing shall be able to -separate me- from the love of God which is in Christ Jesus our

Lord."

So, when you see the **sign over my life** that says, **"Under New Management"... it simply means that…**

- ✓ **The old management couldn't cut it.**
- ✓ **The old management had some flaws. And Now…**
- ✓ **Under New Management things are going to be different…Because…**

- ▪ **The productivity and profits will rise! (Relationship)**
- ▪ **The Working atmosphere will be more joyful and secure!**
- ▪ **In the church fellowship, 'victory In The Lord" will saturate the atmosphere!**

In the same vein,

- ▪ God will be **'glorified'**,
- ▪ The Saints will be **'edified'** and
- ▪ The Devil will be **'horrified'**!

“Under New Management”

Dr. Joseph R. Rogers, Sr., Servant Leader
Mount Zion First Baptist Church
Rocky Mount, North Carolina 27804

<u>“A Charge To Keep: A God To Glorify”</u>

A Sermon By Dr. Joseph R. Rogers, Sr.
For The Morning World Harvest Church
Raleigh, North Carolina 27610
Theme: God's Servant Appreciated
October 29, 2017

<u>Scripture</u>: "And He gave some, **Apostles**; and some, **Prophets**; and some, **Evangelists**; and some, **Pastor and Teachers**. For the **‘perfecting of the Saints’**, for the **‘work of the Ministry’**, for the **‘Edifying of the body of Christ”**. **(Ephesians 4:11, 12)**

Charge = duty, responsibility, or care
Perfecting = Maturing
Work = Action,
Edifying = Building up

<u>Introduction</u>

As we come tonight in **‘celebration’** and **‘honor’** of God’s Servant, I am elated to share this moment with you, Pastor Brunson & Lady Brunson. The ministry of Pastor & First Lady is a **‘high’** and **‘respectable’** assignment, of which, should never be taken lights.

The Pastoral Ministry is an assignment that I have been privileged to serve in for **over forty (40) years**, and on this journey, I have seen the **'worst'** of them and I have seen the **'best'** of them.

- There have been **bad times** and…
- There have been **good times**.
- There have been **sad times** and…
- There have been **joyful times**…BUT…

Through all of **these experiences**, I must say that the Lord has in each case, arisen me as:

- **Victor and never victim!**
- **The Head and never the tail!**
- **Up and never down!**
- **Highly Favored and never cursed!**
- **Above and never beneath!**

In this passage of Scripture, we find the role of pastor/teacher. A duty and a task that carry with it some **'tears'**, **'late night praying'**, **'pain'** and **'agony'**, but because of the power and love of God, there will be times of **‘joy’ ‘peace’** and **‘rewards’.**

The duty of the pastor in today’s church is a very **tedious** and **challenging** experience. Why? Because people are more knowledgeable specifically in **carnal things**, than **spiritual things**.

The bible couches in like this, “People will become **‘wiser’** in the secular things, but **‘weaker’** in the things of God.

And along with that—there are so many different **behaviors**, **personalities**, **attitudes**, **spirits** and God knows what else that The Pastor must be **deal with or be confronted**.

While the pastoral ministry is **‘challenging’**, the rewards of the same, **are out of this world**… such as but not limited to:

- ✓ There is nothing more **fulfilling** than to see someone come out of darkness into the marvelous!

- ✓ There is nothing more **jubilating** than to see someone who thought that life was not living get a new least of life!

- ✓ There is nothing more **rewarding** than to see someone who was once down, now leap to the joy deliverance!

- ✓ There is nothing is more **thrilling** than to see someone who was a babe in Christ, mature and be, all that God would have them to be.

In this process, the **'pastor-shepherd'** plays a vital, integral and important role. The pastor is a **nourisher**, **provider**, **encourager**, and **a leader**, by example and precept. The text suggests, God **sets** (places, parks, position) pastors in the local church fellowship.

But, also in this leadership process, it is the responsibility of that local congregation to **‘listen to’ and ‘follow after”** the man/woman of God as he/she **followers The Lord Jesus Christ.**

The bible says, “[14] **How then shall they call on him in whom they have not believed? and how shall they believe in him of whom they have not heard? and how shall they hear without a preacher**?” **(Romans 10:14)**

What does it mean to be a pastor? The Greek it refers to that of a Shepherd who **looks after, steering and guide the flock**. Again, the Pastor –**guides-, -protects-, and –provider**- the flock with the necessary **-spiritual food**- that’s needed for **–growth- -development**- and –maturity-.

The task of a pastor in the local congregation of believers is very **‘crucial’** and **‘demanding’**. The pastor is a **Servant Leader**! That is, one who **“Serves”**; and put more elementary, one who **waits tables! It is a Charge Without The Possibility of Being Discharged!**

- ✓ **It does not matter how perplexed you become! Remember…**
- ✓ **It does not matter how despaired you may feel!**
- ✓ **It does not matter how far others cast you down!**
- ✓ **It does not matter if others forsake you!**

The Apostle Paul couches in like this in **2 Corinthians 4:1-7:**

"[1] Therefore seeing we have **this ministry**, as we have **received mercy**, we faint not; [2] But **have renounced** the hidden things of dishonesty, not walking in craftiness, nor handling the word of God deceitfully; but by **manifestation of the truth** commending ourselves to every man's conscience in the sight of God.

[3] But if our gospel be hid, it is hid to them that are lost: [4] In whom the god of this world (Satan) hath blinded the minds of them which believe not, lest

the light of the glorious gospel of Christ, who is the image of God, should shine unto them.

5 For we preach not ourselves, but
Christ Jesus the Lord; and ourselves your
servants for Jesus' sake. 6 For God, who
commanded the light to shine out of
darkness, hath shined in our hearts, to
give the light of the knowledge of the
glory of God in the face of Jesus Christ.
7 But we have this **treasure** (anointing) in
earthen vessels, that the excellency of
the power may be of God and not of us"

God has **ordained** you for this office and its responsibilities that can only be carried out **with** His "**Grace**" and "**Strength**". As Pastor (Servant Leader) you you will have to deals with:

****Many different personalities, attitudes, and problems,**

****Mid week service with 10% of the congregation present,**

**Leading with a few actually following,

**Loving while others spewing hate,

**Attempting to organize with some rebelling,

**Trying to be positive while some condemn,

**Praying while some are gossiping,

The Prophet Jeremiah said, "And I (God) will set up **-Shepherds-** over them which shall **feed them**: and they shall **fear no more**, nor be **dismayed**, neither shall **they be lacking**, saith the Lord" **(23:4)**.

The Apostle Luke said in **Acts 20:28**- "Take heed therefore unto yourselves and to al the flock, over the which the -**Holy Ghost**- hath -made- you **overseers (Bishops)**, to **-feed-** the Church of God, which He (God) hath purchased with His own blood".

The Apostle Paul said in **Romans 8:30**-"Moreover whom He did -predestinate-, them he also -called-: and who he –called-, them he also –justified-: and whom he –justified-, them he also –glorified-."

As Pastor you are expected to be a: **Social Worker, Guidance Counselor, Teacher, Preacher, Sounding Board** and **everything else** that is needed to keep the ship afloat and sailing.

In reality, the Pastor is a **normal individual**: Pastors, **Fills Hurt, Cries Real Tears, and Laughs**. Moreover, the Pastorship entails **"stress", "aggravation", and "scrutiny'** just for preaching the Gospel of Jesus Christ. The Devil is out to stop all pastors in their tracks—and because this the congregation must:

- Always **prayer for your pastor,**
- Always **lift your pastor up before the Lord,**
- Always **Encourage your pastor,**
- Always **support your pastor**,

Exposition I

So, what are some of the requires that it take to be an "**Effective Pastor**"? There are at least FIVE (5) CHARACTERISTICS that must be practiced or applied. They can be found in the life of the great Apostle Paul. Let us examine these **characteristics together.**

I. He/She Must Be A Person Of "Confidence": Confidence: assurance; certainty

A. In his/her Salvation.
(I know whom I have believed)

B. In his/her Calling To Preach.
(Damascus road experience)

C. In his/her Placement.
(Persecution he endured)

II. He/She Must Be A Person Of "Convictions": Convictions: belief, godly principles

**Concerning Salvation.
(only through Jesus)
**Concerning the Scriptures.

(no errors)

**Concerning the Sanctuary.
(holy ground)

III. He/She Must Be A Person Of "Commitment". Commitment: duty, responsibility

A. To God.
(putting Him first)

B. To Family.
(taking care of them; leading and steering' helping)

C. To Church.
(being an example)

IV. He/She Must Be A Person Of "Compassion". Compassion: forgiveness, tenderness, mercy

A. Must love God.
B. Must love Family.
C. Must love Fellowman.
D. Must love Church.

V. He/She Must Be A Person Of "Communication".Communication: interaction, conversation

A. The Message of God's Principles.
B. The message of God's Love.
C. The message of God's Judgment.

Conclusion

So, as I close this message, I bid you, **Pastor Marchall Brunson,** God's Servant; **God's Speed, blessings**, and favor.

You must continue to **trust in the Lord with all of your heart God** and **lean not upon your own understanding, but in all your way acknowledge God and He will direct your pathway.**

It is going as you may already know, a little **'rough and tough'** sometimes, but Lord will never, I say **never, leave thee, nor forsake thee—Always, He is nigh Thee!**

- This ministry will get **'overbearing' sometime'**, but the Lord will give you strength!

- This ministry will get **‘discouraging’ sometime**, but the Lord will lift up your spirit!

- This ministry will get **’aggravating sometimes’**, but the Lord will give you peace of mind!

There is one thing that I can **assure you of and that is**:

1 The Lord is your light and your
salvation; whom shall you fear? the Lord
is the strength of your life; of whom
shall you be afraid?

2 When the wicked, even your enemies
and your foes, came upon you to eat up
your flesh, they stumbled and fell.
3 Though an host should encamp against
you, your heart shall not fear: though
war should rise against you, in this will
you be confident.
4 One thing you desired of the Lord,
that will you seek after; that you may
dwell in the house of the Lord all the

days of my life, to behold the beauty of the Lord, and to enquire in his temple.

5 For in the time of trouble he (God) shall hide you in his pavilion: in the secret of his tabernacle shall he hide me; he shall set you up upon a rock.

6 And now shall you head be lifted up above your enemy's round about you: therefore, will you offer in his tabernacle sacrifices of joy; you will sing, yea, you will sing praises unto the Lord.

Because, when the Devil desires to: **Shipwreck your minds, Dampen your spirit, Discourage your thought pattern, hamper your faith, and Steal your JOY!**

Pastor, continue to **call Upon The Lord's Mighty and Power name**! When you do, God will continue to give you the "**power**" and "**ability**" to: "**Cry loud, spare not, and lift up your voice like a trumpet, show Israel their transgressions and Jacob their sins**".

In This **Process of Maintaining** and Doing Ministry continue to have:

- **The Leadership of a Moses,**
- **The Courage of a Joshua,**
- **The Fortitude of an Elijah,**
- **The Mindset of an Ezekiel,**
- **The Compassion of an Isaiah,**
- **The Fortitude of a Nehemiah**
- **The Fire and Boldness of a Jeremiah,**
- **The Wisdom of a Solomon,**
- **The Loud Voice of a John The Baptist,**
- **The Aggressiveness and boldness of a Peter,**
- **The Spiritual Intellect of a Paul,**
- **The Endurance of a John, but most of all…**
- **The Love of a Jesus Christ,**

Stand up when others choose to sit down,

Speak up when others choose to be silent,

Pray when others are gossiping,

- **Follow God** when others choose to turn back on Him,
- **Trust God** when others choose to lose faith in Him,
- Seek God when others choose to distrust Him!

Because, Sheep are known for **wandering**, but as a **Good Shepherd** watch over and guide them on this journey—God will **strengthen you.**

The Apostle Paul couches it like this, **"How then shall they call on Him (Jesus) in whom they have not believed? And how shall they believe in Him who they have not heard. And how shall they hear without a preacher? And how shall they preach, except they be sent".**

<u>**"A Charge To Keep: A God To Glorify"**</u>

Dr. Joseph R. Rogers, Sr., Servant Leader
Morning Star World Harvest Church
Raleigh, NC 27610

<u>"It's All Working For Our Good"</u>
A Sermon By Dr. Joseph R. Rogers, Sr.
For Mount Zion First Baptist Church
Rocky Mount, North Carolina 27804
Theme: A Break Through God
October 29, 2017

<u>Scripture</u>" "And we know that **'all'** things work together for **'good'** to them that **'love'** God and are **'the called'** according to his purpose." **(Romans 8:28)**

<u>Introduction</u>

Have you ever **awakened** in the morning and for a few moments, thought about how far you have come in life? That is, just how much the Lord has **'favored'** and **'bless'** you, even though you are so undeserving of His **'love'** and **'mercy'**?

It is nothing wrong with **reflecting (looking back for a moment)** and taking a **serious look** at how far God has **bought** us through our dangerous **"toils and snares"**!

Through all of it, we should be able to see the **"handiwork" (working, favor)** of **The Great God of Creation 'ruling'** and **'super ruling'** in the midst of our life's **difficulties, challenges** and **threats.**

It is during these challenges days that we join in with the **heavenly choir** and sing the words of the old song by the **"Mighty Clouds of Joy"**, ***"It's been another day's journey and I'm glad about it, I am so glad to be here."***

As we glance back on our journey through **'hindsight' (retrospect, observation)** we can see the long **meandering path** that was laid before us, for the purpose of **disciplining** and **maturing** us. It is without a doubt that…

We remember those **mountains and valleys** of challenge and disappointment.

We remember those **deserts** that were dry and desolate, that we thought we'd never make it through.

We remember those **rivers and streams** that appeared and looked un-crossable.

We remember those **streams of tears** and **rivers of despair** that where had to bear.

When we **look back over our lives** let us **remember** the **high times**, the **joyful times**, the **enriching time** and see the mighty hands of God constantly working things out for us!

When we **climbed higher in live**, we get a panoramic view, which allows you to see **the wider** and **the broader** picture of life and see how **good God 'has been', 'is' and 'will be'** in the future.

Every now and then through this process, we gotten **complacent** and **stop reflecting** and **appreciating** how the mighty hands of God have **worked many situations out** for us.

We must **confess** that, in spite of the challenges, we were able to **see from whence** we have come, and how God did **sustain and preserved us**. In this poster, we also see the results of being chasten by Him.

Let us remember that that is not a process to discourage us, but it is a vehicle for our **pruning**, **tempering** and **maturing** us toward our maturity in the Lord.

As Christians, we must thank God for our **experiences**. We must consider all the **challenges**, **attacks**, **surprises** as God

Mighty Hands **guiding** and **directing** us through **dangerous** and **barren land.**

We must **'understand'** that, though these are **unwanted** and **unwelcomed** challenges, yet, God can **remix them**, even though they bitter, He will make them **sweeter than a Honey Comb.**

- ✓ **We have struggles**, but still all is well!
- ✓ **We valleys of despair**, but still all is well!
- ✓ **We have rainy days**, ALL IS CONTINUING TO BE WELL.
- ✓

Exposition I

This text finds The Apostle Paul explaining to the Romans the nature of the **Christian experience** as it relates to the **Christian journey**.

This journey is full of 'unwanted' experiences!

This journey is full of 'heartache' and pain!

This journey is full of 'misunder-standings'!

The journey is full of sleepless nights!

Yet, The Apostle Paul explained to the Romans that the **entirety** of a person's life is still a **divinely guided pilgrimage** that moves him toward a **glorious end.**

The entire 8th Chapter of Romans, is believed by some to be one of the most **inspirational verses** of the bible, because they focus on the **"Christian's Need"** and how we are guided by Holy Ghost!

The Apostle Paul notes that we should **concentrate on the end**, rather than the **difficulties** encountered along the way with an **optimist (positive), perspective**, rather than a **pessimism (doom, gloom and doubt).**

This text is **powerfully** and **short**, ***"And we know (ASSURED) that 'all' (every experience) things, work together for 'good' (COME OUT IN OUR FAVOR) to them that 'love' God and are 'the called' according to his purpose."***

These Words **empowers us** such that it enables us to **exclaim** with **"FAITH"** and

"ASSURANCE", as did the The Apostle Paul, **"I am persuaded that NOTHING…shall separate me from the LOVE OF GOD…ETC.)**

With this assurance, we can **lifted** our **voices** as would members of choirs proclaiming ***-"I wouldn't take nothing for my journey now!"***

With this assurance we will **walked** the floor as ushers proclaiming***-"I wouldn't take nothing for my journey now!"***

With this assurance we will **preach** and **teach** the word of God in season and out of season proclaiming--***"I wouldn't take nothing for my journey now!"***

With this assurance we will continue to **give our tithes and offering** building of God's Kingdom on earth proclaiming--***"I wouldn't take nothing for my journey now!"***

To be inclusive of everyone here today, we **ALL should be able to say, "I wouldn't take nothing for my journey now."** Because, all of us, regardless to our personal situation, **"have come too far to turn around now."**

During these times we should lift voices and shout, **"I love the Lord, he heard my cry. Long as I live while trouble rise, I'll hasten to his throne."** Yes, we have come a long way and we continue to march toward Beulah Land!

The Nations of Israel left Egypt and wandered in the wilderness for 40 years, but all of that time God **never left them.** And, on our **"Christian Journey"** as we go through many dangerous **toils** and **snares, God will never leave us.**

Let us **not 'posture'** ourselves as The Nation of Israel who could not see God working in:

- **"Egypt"**,
- **"In The Wilderness"**,
- **"At The Red Sea"**,
- **"Crossing The Jordan"** and **"In The Promised Land" (Canaan).**

All some of them could see was the **"difficulties of the journey"** and not the **Power Of God** moving on their behalf.

- They could not see how **they wore the same clothes for 40 years that never wore out.**

- They could not see God **protected from their enemies despite their own inability to defend themselves**.
- They could not see God providing cool fresh water **despite drought situations.**

- They could not see how **God provided food where there were no Food Lions, Kroger, McDonald, Burger Kings, Olive Garden, or Red Lobster,**

Beloved let us **"see"**, **"understand"** and **"appreciate"** God, and **celebrating with JOY**! Why? Because **unlike Israel**:

- We have **seen** the lighting flashing,
- We have **heard** the thunder roll;
- We have **felt sin breaker** dashing trying to conquer our soul,
- We heard the **voice of Jesus**, bidding us still for fight on;

Why! **He (Jesus) has promised** never, NEVER, NEVER… to leave us! No! Never to leave us alone!

On THIS journey…

- ✓ God has been our **rock in a weary land.**
- ✓ God has been our **shelter in the time of storm.**
- ✓ God has been our **way out of no way.**
- ✓ God has been our **bridge over troubling waters.**

"***It's another day's journey, and I'm glad about it! I am just glad to be here!***"

<u>Conclusion</u>

So, in closing, as we **'review where we have been'**, **how God's hand has wonderfully blessed** and **protected us NOW**, we must understand the fact that:

"And we know that **'all'** things work together for **'good'** to them that **'love'** God and are **'the called'** according to his purpose." For and because of **God goodness**, we must **lift up our voices** in thanksgiving and give God glory, praise and honor!

We see all of the **challenges**, but we refuse to become **weary in well doing**; knowing the Lord is **watching over us** and **guiding us** into **that land where joy shall never end!**

So, let us keep our hands in the hands of **"The Man" (Jesus Christ)** who is able to **still the waters and calms the seas**! In Him (Jesus)…

- We will tell the story of **how God brought us through many dangerous toils and snares?**

- Who will tell the story of how **we marched by faith through hardship and troubles that challenged us?**

Are we willing to **face tomorrow** with confidence and say like Joshua, we refuse to give up, saying, **"As for me and my house, we will serve the Lord!"**

Well, we don't know **"what" tomorrow will bring**, but I do know **"who"** holds my future in His! He neither slumber nor sleeps.

In this life, **there will never be a:**

- **CROSS** that we won't be able to bear;
- **MOUNTAIN** that we won't be able to climb!

- **ENEMY** that we won't be able to defeat;
- **BATTLE** we won't be able to win!
- **DARKNESS** so dark that we won't be able to see the Light!
- **TRIAL** that we can't make it through;
- **TEST** that we won't be able to pass!

What I'm glad to know that as we walk through this **tedious journey**, we don't have to **walk it alone**. Because I know **THE MAN**!

✓ **I know a man**, who had **challenging** and **lonesome experiences, but arose victorious on resurrection morning**!

✓ **I know a man**, who had **no medical license** and **never passed the state exam**; yet he **healed the sick and raised the dead**!

✓ **I know a man**, who has **never been trained in culinary art's,** but He took a Lad's Lunch and fed over four and five thousand men, excluding women and children. And when all had eaten twelve (12) basket full were **leftover!**

- ✓ **I know a man,** who has **never attended a School of Optometry**; but He spit on the ground and made spittle of clay, rub it on a man's eyes and told him to go wash in the Pool of Siloam.

- ✓ **I know a man**, who **never attend a college or university**, but He stood strong in light of the doctors of the law in His days.

- ✓ **I know a man**, who **never attended a medical school**, but just His touch healed a lady with a blood issue.

The Songwriter, postures it like this…

Like a ship that's tossed and driven, battered by an angry sea;

When the storms of life are raging, and their fury falls on me,

I wonder what I have done, that makes this race so hard to run;

Then I say to my soul, take courage, the Lord will make a way somehow. Yes! The Lord will make a way somehow,

Jesus, the Lily of the valley!

Jesus, the Bright and Morning star!

Jesus, my way maker, heart fixer, mind regulator!

Jesus, my way, truth and life!

“It’s All Working For Our Good”

Dr. Joseph R. Rogers, Sr., Servant Leader
Mount Zion First Baptist Church
Rocky Mount, North Carolina 27804

<u>"God's Benefits Package"</u>

A Sermon By Dr. Joseph R. Rogers, Sr.
For The Mount Zion First Baptist Church
Rocky Mount, North Carolina 27804
Theme: Well Secured
August 5, 2017

Scripture: "Praise the LORD, O my soul; all my inmost being, praise his holy name. [2] Praise the LORD, O my soul, and FORGET NOT all his BENEFITS." (Psalm 103:1, 2) (Read Entirety)

<u>Introduction</u>

It is obvious to all who sought, seeing and will seek Job seekers focus not so much on the base salary, but also on the include quality of **"the fringe benefits"** from a prospective employer. '

To name a few: a medical plan, a 401K saving plan, profit sharing, vacation and sick days and the list goes on and on…etc.

Oddly enough, we as Christians tend to 'forget' the "awesome benefits" that the Lord offered unto us, once we accept Him as Lord And Savior. Some believe all we have is just a house, seat or mansion in the Kingdom of God.

I have often in the past and it still probe my mind as to why some people are not concern about the conclusion of life—a right relationship with the Creator.

My brothers and sisters, friendships will cease, marriages will be not more, parting hour will soon reach it conclusion, the games of life will be over—THE ONLY THING THAT IS GOING TO MATTER IS ARE OUR SINS WASHED/COVERED IN/BY THE BLOOD OF THE LAMB!

I am glad and happy to announce today that getting SAVED BY THE BLOOD OF JESUS CHRIST has **'fringe benefits'**, even while we are still occupying planet earth. Some of our greatest scholars have tagged them as being called, "Out of This World".

What are benefits? Well, they are the addons, extras that are not part of the main package. Let's look at God's great benefits package that He has designed for us.

It without a doubt, exceeds anything you'll find anywhere in corporate America or even in the world.

Have you ever heard people say concerning their jobs: "The pay is OK, but the benefits are great?" Well, as believers our benefits package is beyond comprehension.

The Author of this Psalm, King David, (The Dancer) shares with us some important insights as to the blessings of the Lord. Let's look at some of God's wonderful benefits?

1. vs. 3 who [FORGIVES] ALL your SINS! (pardons, exonerates)
•• God is willing to forgive our sins! All of them!

Isaiah 6:7-" [7] And he laid it upon my mouth, and said, Lo, this hath touched thy lips; and thine iniquity is taken away, and thy sin purged"

2. vs. 3 who ... [HEALS] ALL your diseases! (delivers)
•• God is willing to heal all our diseases. All of them!

Jeremiah 8:22a-"[22a] *Is there* no balm in Gilead; *is there* no physician there?

• Many years ago, God healed me of a medically diagnosed lung condition, called, <u>"Acute Sarcoidosis"</u>. Not long after my deliverance it was stated to me, "that's not a bad condition, all you have to do is continue to take your medication and you will be alright".

My response to her was, "I am deliver and totally healed, I do not take medication for that". You should have seen the look on her face—God is the healer of our diseases.

Too often, some people stop at verse three (3) after reading the two awesome benefits of:

(a) forgiveness and
(b) healing. Don't stop there!

3. vs. 4 who [REDEEMS] your life from the PIT! (buy back)

•• Don't ever forget all that the Lord delivered us from our sinful position and made us heirs and joint-heirs.

• Mary Magdalene loved Jesus very much even as an immoral woman (seven devils in her). Jesus delivered her and she remembered the <u>"pit"</u> from which Jesus had redeemed her. That same deliverance that was given to her, is open for all who will come to repentance.

4. vs. 4 who ... [CROWNS] you with LOVE and COMPASSION! (adore)

•• A life-changing thought: God loves us some much that He suffered, bled and die for us! In that, He put into motion a relationship that is 'indescribable'. Jesus places us in a position that Satan is not allowed to pluck us out.

5. vs. 5 who [SATISFIES] your desires with GOOD THINGS so that your youth is renewed like the eagle's! (pleases)

•• Jesus spoke of our heavenly Father ***"giving good gifts*** *to those who ask Him"* (Matthew 7:11). What we must do is: Ask, Seek and Knock! He says also, that if we give sparingly, we will reap the same, but if we give bountifully, we will receive in the same manner.

• To those who are faithful in their tithes and offerings, God says, *"See if I will not throw open the floodgates of heaven and pour out so much blessing that*

you will not have room enough for it"
(Malachi 3:10).

6. vs. 6 The Lord [WORKS] righteousness and justice for all the OPPRESSED. (moves on our behalf)

•• In all that the enemy (Satan) tries to do to us: THAT IS, SIFT US AS WHEAT, KILL, STEAL AND DESTROY US, God said, "Sit right here until I make our enemies of footstools" (a stepping stone to higher heights and deeper depths.

Kings David says in Psalms 27
"1 The Lord is my light and my salvation; whom shall I fear? the Lord is the strength of my life; of whom shall I be afraid?

2 When the wicked, even mine enemies and my foes, came upon me to eat up my flesh, they stumbled and fell.

3 Though an host should encamp against me, my heart shall not fear: though war should rise against me, in this will I be confident.

4 One thing have I desired of the Lord, that will I seek after; that I may dwell in the house of the Lord all the days of my life, to behold the beauty of the Lord, and to enquire in his temple.

5 For in the time of trouble he shall hide me in his pavilion: in the secret of his tabernacle shall he hide me; he shall set me up upon a rock.

6 And now shall mine head be lifted up above mine enemy's round about me: therefore, will I offer in his tabernacle sacrifices of joy; I will sing, yea, I will sing praises unto the Lord.

7. vs. 7 He [MADE KNOWN] his ways to Moses, his deeds to the people of Israel. (shared)

•• Unlike pagan deities, God reveals Himself to His people in wonderful ways:

- In His written Word
- In the prophetic word
- In the Living Word, Jesus
- In His wondrous deeds.

John 16:13 “When...the Spirit of truth comes, He will guide you into all truth.”

2 Corinthians 2:10-“[10] But God has revealed them unto us by his Spirit: for the Spirit searches all things, yea, the deep things of God”.

8. vs. 8 The Lord is [COMPASSIONATE] and GRACIOUS, SLOW TO ANGER, ABOUNDING IN LOVE. (sympathy, concern, consideration)

•• Our God is concern for and cares for us, in that, His arms are not so short, that He will not reach down to pick us up and His ears are not so heavy that He will not hear us. He is always an on-time God!

- full of compassion.

- full of grace.

- slow to anger.

- abounding in agape love.

9. vs. 9 He will [not always accuse], nor will he harbor his

ANGER FOREVER. (be critical toward)

• When God forgives sins (vs. 3), they are forgotten. God puts them in the seas of forgetfulness, never to remember them anymore. God never hold things over our heads.

10. vs. 10 He does not [treat us] as our SINS DESERVE or repay us according to our iniquities. (actions of love and grace)

•• This is an act that see us through the Blood of Jesus Christ! I am glad that God does not give us what we deserve--judgment and punishment, but He washes and sanctifies us—and in the process, He *wipes the slate clean! What does God do…*

11. vs. 12 As far as the [east is from the west], so far has he REMOVED OUR TRANSGRESSIONS from us.

A biblical description of what God does is…

• He casts our sins behind His back (Isaiah 38:17) ...

• He throws them in the depths of the sea (Micah 7:19) ...

• He makes our scarlet sins white as snow (Isaiah 1:18) ...

• He remembers them no more (Hebrews 8:12).

12. vss. 17-18 But from [EVERLASTING TO EVERLASTING] the LORD's LOVE is with those who fear him, and his righteousness with their children's children". (Eternal Relationship)

• God's love and all these benefits from Him are not fickle, (inconsistent, unpredictable, erratic) and fleeting (brief, short-lived, momentary).

• No! God will 'love us' and 'be faithful' to these promises *"from everlasting to everlasting." God has PROMISED…*

That He would never to leave us nor forsake us!

That no weapons that formed itself against would prosper!

That He would hide us in His pavilion.

That good and mercy would follow us all the days of our lives!

That if we tithe, windows would be open unto us!

That He would come to our rescue in times of trouble!

These PORMISES, my brothers and sister, go even to our children, Grandchildren and down to the fourth generation—nothing but BLESSINS!

Conclusion

God's Benefits Package! FULL OF Blessings and Promises? Well…A promise is a <u>commitment</u> to do something. God's Blessings (Promises) are:

- Forgiveness of sins,
- Healing of diseases,
- Deliverance from troubles,
- Divine love and compassion,
- Good things to us,
- Justice for the oppressed.
- Divine compassion, grace patience, and love to us,
- Forgetting our sins,

- Restraining His just anger,
- Removal of our transgressions

... **<u>God Has Promised…</u>**

To supply every need we have.

That His grace is sufficient for us.

That His children will not be overtaken with temptation.

Us victory over death.

That all things work together for good to those who love and serve Him faithfully.

That those who believe in Jesus and are baptized for the forgiveness of sins will be saved and enjoy eternal life.

…And to add icing to the cake, God guarantees that He will be all these things to us *"from everlasting to everlasting"*.

"God's Benefits Program"

Dr. Joseph R. Rogers, Sr., Servant Leader
Mount Zion First Baptist Church
Rocky Mount, North Carolina 27804

II. The Author's Contact Information and Other Works

A. Mailing Address:
(919) 208-0200

B. Email Address:
jroger3420@aol.com

HOW TO WALK
IN YOUR DESTINY
"YOUR PATHWAY
TO VICTORY"
DR. JOSEPH R.
ROGERS, SR.

MY ROLE IN
THE LOCAL
CHURCH
STAY IN
YOUR LANE
UNITY
DR. JOSEPH ROOSEVELT
ROGERS SR.

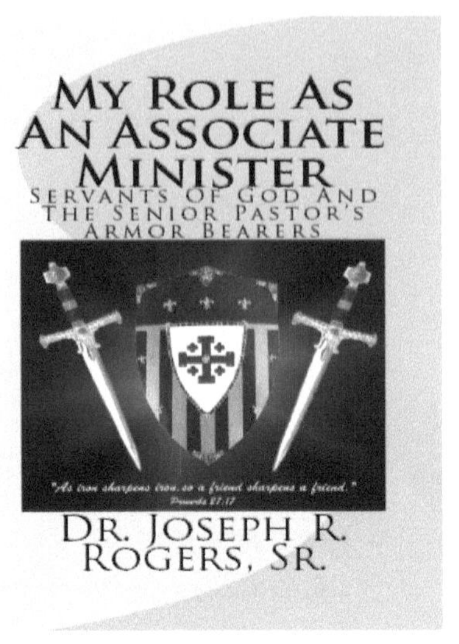
My Role As
An Associate
Minister
Servants Of God And
The Senior Pastor's
Armor Bearers
"As iron sharpens iron, so a friend sharpens a friend."
Proverbs 27:17
Dr. Joseph R.
Rogers, Sr.

Christian
Discipleship And
The Holy Spirit
Equipping And Empowering
For Kingdom Building
Holy Spirit
Dr. Joseph R Rogers Sr.

A STUDY OF THE
BOOK OF PSALMS
STUDY SERIES L
UNDERSTANDING THE
HYMNS OF THE BIBLE
THE
PSALMS
WHAT TO DO
WITH OUR
FEARS TEARS
GUILT
DEPRESSION
DESIRES JOY
DR. JOSEPH ROOSEVELT
ROGERS, SR.

MARRIAGE
GOD'S WAY
"KEEP THE FIRE
BURNING"
DR. JOSEPH R. ROGERS, SR.

CHURCH
LEADERSHIP
THE PASTOR AND
THE DEACON
GOD
DR. JOSEPH R. ROGERS SR.

My Role As
A Church
Trustee
THE KEEPER OF
GOD'S HOUSE
DR. JOSEPH ROOSEVELT
ROGERS, SR.

EVANGELISM
101
"TEARING DOWN THE
KINGDOM OF DARKNESS"
DR. JOSEPH R ROGERS SR.

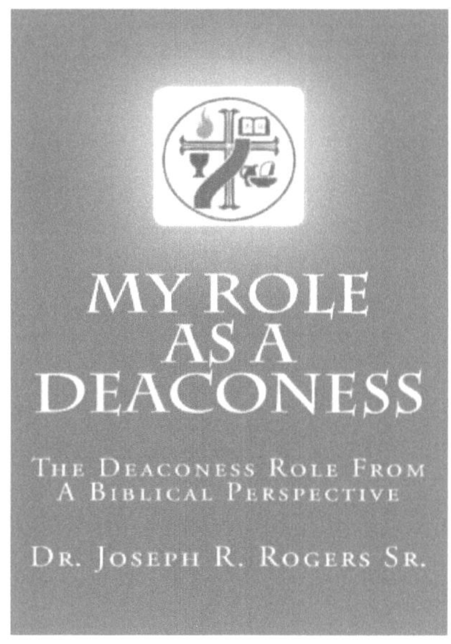
MY ROLE
AS A
DEACONESS
THE DEACONESS ROLE FROM
A BIBLICAL PERSPECTIVE
DR. JOSEPH R. ROGERS SR.

(There Is A Series of 1-54)

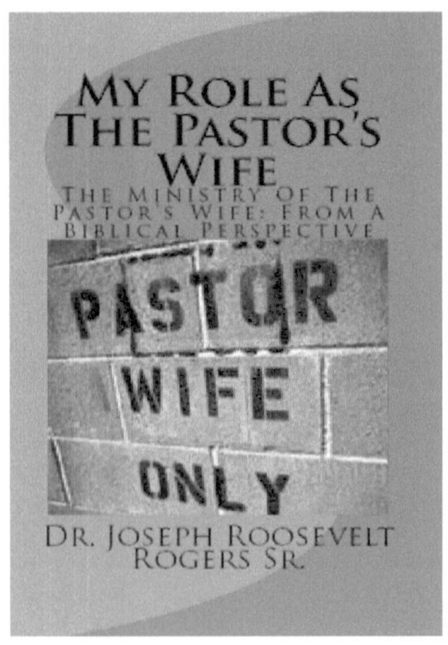

MY ROLE
AS A
DEACON
THE DEACON'S ROLE: FROM
A BIBLICAL PERSPECTIVE
DR. JOSEPH R. ROGERS, SR.

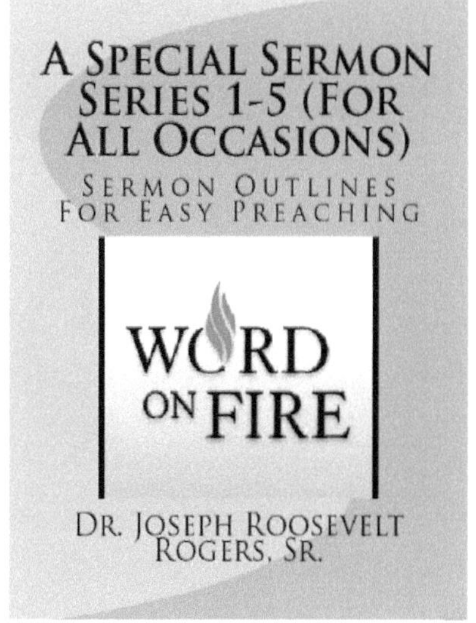
A SPECIAL SERMON
SERIES 1-5 (FOR
ALL OCCASIONS)
SERMON OUTLINES
FOR EASY PREACHING
WORD
ON FIRE
DR. JOSEPH ROOSEVELT
ROGERS, SR.

DIVORCE
GOD'S WAY
(FROM A
BIBLICAL
PERSPECTIVE)
Trust God..Pick Up The
Pieces..And Move Forward
Dr. Joseph R. Rogers Sr.

My Role As
A Christian
Missionary
Equipping And
Engaging In The
Missionary Ministry
God's Work
Our Hands
Dr. Joseph Roosevelt
Rogers, Sr.

RENEWING YOUR
MIND: SPIRITUAL
INVENTORY
DR. JOSEPH R. ROGERS, SR.

MEN'S DAY
SERMON
OUTLINES S
SERMON OUTLINES
FOR EASY PREACHING
A few
good men
DR. JOSEPH R.
ROGERS, SR.

BLESSED AND HIGHLY FAVORED A STUDY SERIES: PHYSICAL & SPIRITUAL BLESSINGS
Dr. Joseph Rogers, Sr.

"THE DAYS OF OUR YEARS ARE THREESCORE YEARS AND TEN; AND IF BY REASON OF STRENGTH THEY BE FOURSCORE YEARS". (PSALMS 90:10A)
Graceful Seniors
MINISTERING TO THE SENIORS
Understanding The Myths & Truths Of The Aging Process
DR. JOSEPH R. ROGERS SR.

III. Notes:

NOTE CON'T...

www.ingramcontent.com/pod-product-compliance
Ingram Content Group UK Ltd.
Pitfield, Milton Keynes, MK11 3LW, UK
UKHW041934190726
13854UKWH00004B/1590